10 STEPS
TO CREATING AN
EMPOWERING
LEGACY

10 STEPS
TO CREATING AN
EMPOWERING LEGACY

**How to Build
Multi-Generational Wealth
and Empower Loved Ones
to their Full Potential!**

FUQUAN BILAL

Printed in the United States of America.
First paperback edition July 2022.

Cover design by Mocah Studio, LLC.
Layout design by G Sharp Design, LLC.

ISBN 979-8-9864816-6-1

Contents

Preface vii

Introduction 1

01   Know Your Priorities 7

Turning Priorities into Specific, Tangible Goals 8

02   Acknowledge and Own the Gaps 15

Where Are You Now? 16

What Are You on Track to Do? 19

How Big Is the Void? 19

Where Do You Need to Catch Up? 20

Taking Ownership 22

03   The Biggest Threats 23

Lack of Action 24

Taxes 25

Time 26

Bad Investments 30

Posthumous Asset Management 31

04   Five Vehicles for Facilitating Your Goals . . 35

Wills 36

IRAs 37

Trusts 39

Real Estate 40

Funds 41

05 **Make Introductions Now** **43**

Start By Having the Conversation 44

Making Introductions 46

06 **Put Them in Charge of the Money** **49**

Test Accounts 50

Bank Accounts and Credit Cards 50

Create a Family Bank 52

Family Gifts 53

Reward Systems 53

07 **Teach Them** **55**

Books 56

Alternatives to Books 56

Other Forms of Education 58

08 **Train Them** **59**

Raising Your Kids to Be Investors and Entrepreneurs 60

Instilling a Passion for Important Causes .... .61

Training Others 62

09 **Make Wise, Future-Proof Investments Now** **65**

7 Key Investing Principles for Maximizing Your Legacy.... 66

10 **Create Your To-Do List** **71**

Putting it into Action 72

Conclusion **75**

About the Author................... **77**

About NNG **79**

Preface

Those who know me often describe me as a pragmatic optimist. I'm always optimistic and looking at how even the most challenging events can be used and navigated for more positive outcomes. I'm also a realist, and keenly aware of and familiar with the fact that things just aren't going to fix and take care of themselves, so I am not immune from thinking about the future. I want my kids to be taken care of and equipped to succeed if and when anything happens to me — for them to be able to explore the opportunities that come their way and to live to their full individual potential. That might include taking care of their own families, grandchildren, and other people around them as well.

These are the factors in life that I have found keep the most people up at night; the concerns that fill their heads and keep them awake, rolling around, trying to find the headspace to sleep and solve these concerns at the same time.

For many more, this kind of focus is what gets them out of bed in the morning, especially when they don't feel like it. Knowing that others depend on them and that their work isn't done pulls them out of the covers, makes them put their feet on the floor, and pushes them to the kitchen for whatever wakes them up for work.

This book isn't just about kids, although they may be one of the most compelling examples. It can also apply to your spouse, partner, parents, pets, and even others in your community and around the world whom you care about passionately.

For some, ensuring wealth and financial security may be more about causes than individual members of the immediate family. Maybe what scares and drives you the most is the environment, your faith, or a pending crisis. You may be propelled to create a legacy, perhaps not just for your own ego, but to have the maximum possible impact, leave the world a better place, or at least leave some bread crumbs of inspiration and leadership that others can grasp and follow through on.

I want to help with that. It is why I invested in writing and sharing this book. With this book, I share both my personal experiences of how I've decoded some of the processes and financial steps to creating a legacy and empowering the next generation, and some of the tools I've picked up and learned from other experts in related fields for facilitating and protecting your efforts. Most of all, I talk about how to turn worrying into doing and getting results so you can sleep well and be confident in your plan and what you've put into place. So you wake up eager to get out of bed because you are excited about the future — not just to clock in at work and hope you find a few pennies left over at the end of the month.

This is for you, even if you have a solid, high-paying job with a prestigious title, but you know you could be doing a lot better with creating and leaving a legacy and empowering others. Even if you've built great wealth, but you don't have a concrete, future-proofed financial or succession plan yet. Especially if you are just starting out in the workforce and want to optimize your time.

I will tell you that once you start focusing on the advice in this book, you may be surprised at the change you effect in others. It was one of my young sons who came up with the idea of becoming the bank during the Great Recession, which led to starting a revolution in the mortgage note business that drove this home for me. Once you light the right fires, they can go on to have a fantastic ripple effect across generations.

This book contains keys that you can begin implementing immediately, *today*.

I also have the vision that your kids and grandkids, neighbors' kids, and people in other countries will one day find this book on your shelves and theirs, and be greatly empowered by it.

Introduction

What's the big problem? Not taking that first step.

Sure, a lot of things can keep you busy and distracted from what's really important today. Just check your phone for notifications one more time, or refresh the inbox on your laptop. It's easy to find a few more moments of mental detour to keep you from thinking about what really matters, and from actually doing something about it.

If you'd like to stop worrying or wishing, and want to start living, then this book is for you.

Whether you are frustrated at not getting traction in a certain area, aren't at peace with a current situation or the future, aren't confident about your plan and setup, or just want to do better, these pages will help. And once you start putting these easy steps into action, I am confident you will find what you need, and the results will be energizing. You'll want to share them with others.

Most of us consider how we can prepare for and champion what's next. We yearn to do more, provide for others, and empower them to be their best.

For some, this might mean wanting to provide the basics and necessities for kids or other close family members. For others, it is about enabling those loved ones to have freedom and equipping them with the knowledge, resources, and skills to make it on their own, and to live out their full potential and have a full and enjoyable life. This can apply to your spouse, partners, siblings, neighbors, people who work for you, or others who may be disadvantaged whom you want to help and give the chance to succeed. It could also be a cause that you deeply care about.

However, despite all the time these thoughts consume, few take real action on them, even among the apparently successful and highly intelligent. Few set it up. Very few do it well.

The result is coming in far short of aspirations and hopes, causing years of unnecessary stress and other negative impacts, including being robbed of your precious time. Even those who have gotten ahead well financially often find that their resources are quickly lost or wasted. But it doesn't have to be that way

THE TRUTH EVERYONE NEEDS TO KNOW

The bottom line is that the average, the status quo, and even the high side of that by following all the conventional advice will not deliver for you or those you care about. You don't have to believe only me. Here are the numbers you need to know.

An individual's median savings in America, according to ValuePenguin,[1] reached just over $5,000 pre-pandemic. That was less than the average savings in 2001. Even by age 75, the median savings was only around $9,000. Not a lot to show for a lifetime of work and investing. Not much of a legacy to leave. Funeral expenses alone would

---

1   https://www.valuepenguin.com/banking/average-savings-account-balance.

mean most people will leave their loved ones with debt and eat up their savings, instead of leaving them anything to live and prosper on.

However, these numbers are often very misleading. What they leave out is that many don't even have savings accounts at all, leaving the true average savings amount probably closer to $400, according to some bankers and financial analysts.

According to the Federal Reserve,[2] median savings fell to just $3,500 post-COVID, with 39% not having enough to cover a $400 emergency. That isn't even enough to change tires on a car, pay half a month of rent, or get a tooth pulled.

Also according to the Federal Reserve,[3] the individual median net worth in America pre-COVID was $121,760. Again, the true average is probably in the negative.

That may seem like a lot, but many people are surprised at how fast they burn through this money once they retire. It is not uncommon to burn through 50% of savings in just the first five years of retirement. If you've saved $1M for retirement and you retire at 70 years old, you could be down to $500k by the time you are 75. If you live until you are 95, that's going to be a struggle. When you factor in inflation, that money may buy just 10% of what it does today.

Can you live on $2,500 a year? A $1M goal won't get you through your own retirement. Not by a long way. And forget about having anything left over for anyone else.

At the time of writing this, the Social Security Administration[4] deemed 67 years old as the "normal retirement age." Many people

---

2   https://www.fool.com/the-ascent/research/average-savings-account-balance/.

3   https://www.federalreserve.gov/econres/scf/dataviz/scf/chart/#series:Net_Worth;dem ographic:all;population:all;units:mean;range:1989,2019

4   https://www.ssa.gov/oact/progdata/nra.html.

believe they can keep on working until they are 70 to make up for a lack of retirement and legacy planning.

According to Experian[5], the *real* average age that people retire is 62. This is often due to being laid off or becoming too sick to work, not because people can afford to retire early. If you planned to do all your saving and investing late in life, between age 62 and 70, guess what? Chances are you won't have anything. If you happen to be part of the small group who does very well in building up an inheritance to leave behind, you will see most of that immediately lost if you don't have intelligent and intentional estate planning in place.

Heirs may pay 3% or more of the estate to lawyers to figure it all out. Even if you've done well, estate taxes and inheritance taxes may apply. At a federal level, this has been around 40%, although the current (2022) administration and president hope to raise that to 61%. Each state has its own taxes of these types, too. If you're keeping your money in Maryland, for instance, both estate taxes and inheritance taxes will apply on anything you plan to leave for your loved ones.

Even if something is left after all that, between 30% to 70% of heirs completely blow their inheritances. That's 7 out of 10. You don't get to be the slim exception by chance.

What is really ironic, or tragic, is that the vast majority work their entire lives in near misery for this sad outcome. According to Salary.com,[6] only around 38% of people are fulfilled by their

5   https://www.experian.com/blogs/ask-experian/
     average-retirement-age/#:~:text=Among%20the%20respondents%20to%20
     Gallup's,planned%20to%20retire%20was%2064.

6   https://parade.com/227302/viannguyen/only-38-percent-of-americans-fee
     l-fulfilled-by-their-work-more-survey-results/.

work. Most people are living "lives of quiet desperation," and aren't seeing much in the way of results. In fact, 54% of those surveyed say they would be willing to take a job for less money if they could do something they love.

According to one hospice nurse,[7] the deathbed regret of every single male patient she ever took care of was working too much and not having enough time to be with their children or partners.

It is glaringly clear that most people are not only poorly financially prepared for retiring, but even less so for leaving a financial legacy. Even when they do, it is usually wasted and lost. Most die unhappy, even though they may have worked hard, saved a lot, put money in 401ks, and listened to big financial institutions' ads and brokers. It doesn't have to be that way.

I WANT BETTER FOR YOU

This book will set you on a better trajectory — one that is fulfilling and can deliver extraordinary results.

We will go from establishing goals and a game plan that will cover and provide for what's most important to how to bridge any gaps and the void between where you are now and where your approaches have let you down. You'll learn the biggest threats to your hopes and aspirations, as well as the tools you need to put in place to defeat them.

In the second half of the book, we'll walk through the most powerful and effective ways to put your finances in place, along with the skills and know-how you need so your beneficiaries can start benefiting right now, will be ready in advance, and will be able to

---

7   https://www.oldcolonyhospice.org/blog/bid/101702/nurse-reveals-the-top-five-regret
s-people-make-on-their-deathbed.

enjoy all that you want for them. Plus, exactly how to start putting them into action *today*.

It's your GPS to success, financial peace, and the right structures for the optimal net result.

Dive into easy steps to start working on, with long-term compounding results. Don't put off until tomorrow what you can do today. Tomorrow is never promised, and there is no telling what may happen the day after tomorrow.

After all, this is the one thing — the most important thing with the biggest possible impact — you can take action on. And the sooner you solve it, the better.

Chapter 1

KNOW YOUR PRIORITIES

"Your priorities aren't what you say they are. They are revealed by how you live."

You are reading this because you feel that building wealth for yourself and those you love is important to you. You are also reading it because either you haven't taken real, meaningful action and progress on your priorities yet, or what you have tried hasn't worked enough.

Yes, you may have been busy. We are all busy. Everyone is busy. Yet no one is too busy. It is just a matter of priorities. People will always find time for the things they really want to do, no matter what. No matter how urgent some things may seem sometimes, Rick Warren says, "If your activities don't match your priorities, you are wasting your life."

The first step to success is knowing your priorities. "When you know what's most important to you, making a decision is simple," says Tony Robbins.

Once you have this clarity about your priorities and are equipped with the details of this book, it will be much simpler to create what you want. When you take action on those priorities, that's when good things will happen.

TURNING PRIORITIES INTO SPECIFIC, TANGIBLE GOALS

What we sometimes refer to as "priorities" are often nothing more than vague, fluffy ideas. These are not very actionable or achievable. This is true no matter how noble or important they are. It is said that a dream without a goal is just a wish. A goal without a plan just becomes a dream.

The way to break through this, and make tangible progress and get results, is to turn your priorities into specific, tangible goals. Only then can you map your way toward them and create a short list of actionable to-do items that are real priorities.

What are your priorities?

What is really most important to you is often revealed in your worst fears and concerns, as well as your desires and the things that you want most passionately.

A dream may represent a future outcome. A goal is action-oriented. Goals are specific, with details and deadlines.

An example of this difference would be "I dream of my kids being financially set when I pass on, so they can focus on pursuing their own passions and can take chances on opportunities that come along, instead of being stuck in the rat race" versus "I want to be able to provide my family $2,000 per month and a free and clear home with no payments within five years, so after I die, they can focus on having a positive impact on the world with their unique talents."

The details are up to you. The specifics are unique to you. It could just as easily be ensuring your favorite puppy is provided a pampered and luxurious lifestyle for the rest of their life. Or to fund education and a business startup budget for 100 young people a year. Or to ensure safe drinking water for a billion people. What matters is defining your goals or priorities, not what they might be. Let's start clarifying and putting these parts together to create your own goals.

Start with Who or What

Who or what is it that you want to help with your legacy and life's work? While it may be tempting to start rattling off a whole list of people and causes, this exercise, and how effective it will be, relies on simplicity and clarity. Start with who or what is most important to you.

Don't worry — along the way, you will find ways to expand your impact. After you've accomplished your top-priority goal, you can go on to set additional expansion goals and go even further and bigger. Yet that all relies on being very focused right now.

Who or what is most important?

It can be a spouse, child, family member, friend, pet, group of people, or cause. Write it down, or type it into the notes on your phone.

How Much?

Your desires and wishes for your "who or what" may not be focused on money. They may initially be about comfort, safety, freedom, and opportunity. These are your purpose.

Those are hard terms to be specific about. Most of them, fortunately, can be converted into monetary terms in some way.

This may certainly require factoring in inflation, but it is doable, and necessary.

You can put a dollar figure on them, including how much it would cost to be taken care of if you no longer have the mental or physical capacity to do so, or to work and earn any longer. You can do it for the level of basic sustenance and comfort versus work and motivation to work you want to leave for your heirs. You can price out specific projects and ventures.

To be sure you aren't a burden that eats up your legacy and nest egg, start with that number. Then multiply how much support you want to provide and for how long, and what it should provide for your who or what. Be prepared for a bit of a shock: That amount will probably be a lot more than you thought or expected to need to save and build up for with investments so far.

This number will be absolutely critical as the foundation for everything else.

Take your time here. Write it down.

When?

When do you need to hit these goals?

Perhaps you plan to retire in five years — or not for 20 years. You'll want to be sure that you have built up the passive income to provide for yourself and any other dependents when your earned income ends, as well as some level of nest egg to cover unexpected cash expenses and emergencies, such as medical costs, home maintenance, new vehicles, etc. Put a date on this. This should already be in place at the level you desire before you get there.

Remember that the odds are high that you will end up retiring, and your earned income will end, years before you expect, so be sure to build in a cushion — most retirees end up burning through their nest eggs a lot faster than planned.

The bulk of your legacy may be intended for after you die. It may be about the care and provision you want to leave behind, but you may also want to provide some financial assistance at certain points in others' lives before you're gone — college tuition, the down payment for your child's first home, or seed capital for your kids to start their own businesses.

Make sure to plan for liquidity at these events, too. If one of those events will occur in five or 10 years, you may want to ensure some of your investments mature around those dates, so capital will be available for withdrawal. This will also require certain types of investments.

You don't want to rely on a portfolio of publicly traded stocks to be at a certain value in five or 10 years — they may be in a crisis and virtually worthless, creating massive financial losses if you sell them at that moment.

With all of this in mind, you may have several milestones along your timeline that are part of your goals.

What for?

While we've focused on the monetary part of this so far, it's important to be clear about the "what for."

As we touched on earlier, financial inheritances are frequently wasted, probably more often than not. Purely financial large inheritances may even do more harm than good.

More and more highly intelligent individuals and families have come out to announce that they won't be leaving the bulk of their fortunes to their kids in cash — a stark contrast to the mentality of those who can only dream of being able to leave large cash inheritances behind. They may even make it their life's dream or goal at any costs.

Some of the well-known people who have reportedly pledged not to leave the bulk of their fortunes to their kids include:

- Gordon Ramsay
- Sting
- MacKenzie Scott
- Larry Page
- Mark Zuckerberg
- Michael Bloomberg
- Bill Gates
- Warren Buffett
- Jackie Chan
- Elon Musk

We used to have defined benefit retirement plans. Those were ditched for defined contribution plans. Even Social Security won't save you or provide for your goals. This often means plowing money into plans without any certainty about what you or your heirs will receive later. In contrast, a defined benefit plan focuses on what you want your savings and investments to provide at certain points in your life later on. If you are thinking about a legacy and goals, then you certainly want to focus on predictable benefits. Not only for yourself, but for those you want to help.

Again, this may not be money or a specific dollar amount, but what a legacy can do for them. It might include things like:

- Providing basic food and housing needs
- Paying for investment or business startup costs

- Paying for education and training
- Funding opportunities and personal pursuits
- Having a positive impact on the world
- Leaving landmarks

Create your own list and use it as your compass and motivation.

Chapter 2

ACKNOWLAGE AND OWN THE GAPS

You have to acknowledge a problem exists before you can actually go about finding a solution."—*Demi Moore*

One of the most critical steps in creating a powerful legacy, or just a strong financial future for yourself, is recognizing the gap between where you are now and where you want to be. To get where you want to go, you've got to know what it is going to take.

This may not always be at the top of your fun list, but it can be, given how inspiring and meaningful the end results will be.

Many avoid this effort. Great opportunities are often disguised as work, so many people simply don't go there. It is easier to scroll on

Instagram a little longer or find something to binge-watch on Hulu to distract yourself.

However, acknowledging and owning the gaps in your financial plan can be a relatively simple exercise — one that is mentally stimulating and motivating, especially when you consider that it will be 10 times harder every year *not* to do this, and that not doing so means ending up with poor results. Even more so when you realize that you can't get that time and those years back.

WHERE ARE YOU NOW?

This exercise and step begins with taking inventory of where you are now.

Cash

What is your cash situation — how much cash do you have on hand? That is, cash not already dedicated to bills, regular spending, or floating for expenses between paydays?

How much of an emergency fund do you have? Do you have three to 12 months of expenses in reserve? Are you comfortable with that cushion? Do you also have reserves set aside for other assets that will cost you money sooner or later, like your cars or rental properties you directly own and manage?

How much additional cash savings do you have on top of this? That is money that could be invested instead of sitting idle or going down in value and being eaten up by bank fees.

Net Worth

How much is your net worth? That is all of your cash on hand and the value of your investments and assets, minus your debts and liabilities, not including any homes or real estate that you live in or have for personal use.

This is especially important when it comes to your legacy and the estate you will pass on. Remember that your executor or heirs will have to pay off any debts, including taxes, and will only get what is left over.

That number may be even lower because they will often look to liquidate assets quickly — they often won't hold onto vehicles, homes, or other valuables for six months to try to get the best price, while maintaining any holding costs. They will most likely sell at a discount to liquidate quickly and avoid having money bleed from holding onto them.

Investments

How much do you have in investments?

This may include direct investments in real estate, precious metals, cryptocurrencies, bonds, private company stocks, private funds, retirement accounts, cash value of life insurance plans, and stock market investments.

You will probably have to discount the value of some of these investments, just as a mortgage underwriter would do when calculating them as a part of your assets and liquid assets, to account for volatility and the cost of selling and turning them into usable cash. Some of these investments or assets may have much higher fees or penalties to cash out than others. Factor that in.

Others may be highly volatile, such as public stock investments and bitcoin, which may be subject to valuation swings as much as 25% to 75% in a very short period of time.

How much would you have if you had to sell everything to pass it on today? Or if you had to sell in a down market five years from now?

Passive Income

How much passive income do you have coming in each month? How much of that is consistent ongoing net cash flow that will keep coming in without you having to do anything at all for it?

Consider how much that net income may change with taxes, inflation, and other costs, or any compression in the market that affects that income.

How many streams of passive income do you have in case one or more is disrupted? What percentage of them will you calculate your income on to account for any disruptions — 90%? 75%?

Are these income streams expected to last for the long term — 20 or 30 years, or more? At least as long as you expect to need it, or will the capital supporting it have to be reinvested to renew this income?

Beneficiary Situations

What is the situation (financial and otherwise) of your primary beneficiaries — your individual heirs or the organizations working on the causes you plan to support and empower with your legacy?

How well are they set up to survive, thrive, and take advantage of opportunities between now and when you pass on the bulk of your estate? What is their income-generating ability, exposure to crises, and freedom to pursue their passions and talents to the full?

Have your heirs demonstrated financial savvy and the organizations you care about shown responsible fiscal behavior? They may already be very well-positioned with strong, future-proofed finances. If that's the case, you won't feel you have to take on all the burden of helping them yourself.

They could be facing big gaps now or in the years ahead that mean you want to step up earlier to help.

WHAT ARE YOU ON TRACK TO DO?

Given the math you've done on your assets, net worth, passive income, and other factors, what are you on track for — that is, if you can keep up your current progress, savings, investments, debt reduction, passive income, and rates of return, where are your finances headed?

Are you in a downward spiral that you need to break free from, or are you maintaining positive momentum?

How will either position affect these factors in one, five, 10, 20, and 30 years from now?

Where is your estate headed in 30, 50, and 100 years from now? Break it down and see where your current trajectory is taking you.

Don't forget to factor in volatility. If you only recently started investing in a tremendous bull run, then your average returns over the next 10 years may be substantially lower than if you had been doing so all along.

HOW BIG IS THE VOID?

Looking at where you are currently headed and the timeframe you have in mind, how does that compare to your goals and needs?

You can easily make this comparison by creating a document with two columns to list your cash, net worth, investment account balances, passive income, and estimated estate value.

What is the difference between these columns — most importantly, how far off is your trajectory? If you are not on track to meeting or exceeding your goals, you need to take action.

The sooner you correct your plan and GPS, the easier it will be to improve your position and future; the sooner you will see the results of being on the right path. That is energizing and compelling, and will make you want to do more of it. The longer you wait, the harder it will be to catch up and close this gap, the harder you will have to work, the more hours you will have to work, the more you will have to sacrifice in quality time and as a percentage of your finances, and the riskier the money moves you will have to make to catch up on lost time. That, of course, can derail everything.

Start sooner, and you won't have to take unnecessary risks. When you know you are on the right track, you will sleep better, live better, and be happier. That will have a big impact on those around you, too.

WHERE DO YOU NEED TO CATCH UP?

Break down the individual categories where you need to catch up. Perhaps you are doing well with your cash and emergency fund. That's great, even if you are just on track to meet this goal.

Perhaps your investments are underperforming on ROI and are not going to cut it. Maybe simply improving your returns can put you on the right trajectory. One move might be trading out of low-performing CDs or bonds that are producing 4% or 5% returns, and putting them in still low-risk, but better-performing investments that yield 8% or 10% returns each year.

This difference alone can double your end result. Even based on having $10,000 in capital now and saving $10,000 a year with a 4% annual return versus a 10% return will mean $640,000 instead of just $319,000 over the next 20 years. If you are saving and investing more, you may be talking about millions of dollars in difference.

Passive income will be a very important part of this. Consider whether you might need to move more of your investments to passive income-producing vehicles over time, or at least to diversify into multiple streams of income.

With these other adjustments, you may be able to restructure your portfolio into less-risky investments, which will be more reliable and can be counted on with more confidence later, when you need them the most. (In Chapter 9, we'll dive further into how to make some of these future-proofing investments.)

It is vital to be aware that this process is not just about the money, either. It is also smart to identify any gaps in knowledge. You may see this void and be motivated to get on track and excel, but you might not know exactly how to do so yet — how to find more surplus funds, how to invest them, and how to maximize the impact for your beneficiaries. That's okay. It can all be learned. It won't take a four-year degree or student loan debt, either.

You may also spot gaps in the knowledge of your beneficiaries and be able to transfer appreciation, equip them to do better by themselves now, and maximize anything you pass onto them.

TAKING OWNERSHIP

While a lot of help is out there for you, no one else will do it all for you.

This process should be empowering, not daunting. It can come a lot easier and faster than you think, at least once you start making the right steps in the right direction.

Whether you realize it or not, you are a leader, especially in respect to your legacy and estate. You may be the one to make it, but what happens next, and how effective that is for your children, your grandchildren, or the next generation of socially conscious entrepreneurs, will depend a lot on the way you lead. They may not listen or follow what you say, but they will eventually copy what you do.

As former Navy SEAL Jocko Willink says, "Good leaders don't make excuses. Instead, they figure out a way to get it done." You're already in the right place to do this. Just keep reading.

Chapter 3

THE BIGGEST THREATS

"Don't be fearful of risks. Understand them, and manage and minimize them to an acceptable level."—Naved Abdali

You can feel as if you are making fantastic progress toward your goals, but you can see it all lost and wasted almost in an instant.

This isn't just a problem for individuals and new investors. It has struck many of the wealthiest and most famous, as well as many of the largest and longest-running corporations. We've seen it with companies that have been around for 100 years or valued at tens of billions of dollars, along with Hollywood actors, celebrity athletes, and artists who have lost it all despite making millions of dollars a year.

There are two important parts to this. The first is that you have to work just as hard to protect your gains as to make them. This most commonly becomes an issue when people start out with nothing to lose. They don't have much, so they are willing to take risks and just go, go, go. They may see big results fast — then things implode almost overnight. They forgot to pause, take stock of the progress they had made, and put protections in place.

The second is that it is what you don't know that gets you. As Vincent H. O'Neil said, "Plan ahead for developments that could seriously impact you, and then decide how you'd deal with them." When we anticipate the risks, we can protect ourselves and offset them.

The problem is when we don't know those risks are there. As the manager of financial reporting at Tangerine Bank in Canada has put it, the key is to "understand [the risks], and manage and minimize them to an acceptable level."

Aside from the individual risks unique to specific investments and methods of holding your money and transferring it, what are the overall biggest threats to your plans for your legacy and estate?

LACK OF ACTION

Robert Kiyosaki has said that "the biggest risk a person can take is to do nothing." It's true. It may not feel like it at the time. Some people get frozen by analyzing their options and perceived risks of taking action, even if those risks are small. They rarely calculate the lost opportunity costs, which can be far greater.

These are tangible and very real costs and losses. Just as with the example of investing at different rates of return, if you don't make that improvement, you are losing 50% of what you could have, or more. Instead of $600,000, you will only have $300,000. That's expensive. It gets worse if you fail to invest at all.

You'll end up with less than you started with. It's never too late to start. Every day you wait costs you money, and more hard work to catch up later. Failing to act on other ways to protect your wealth and estate can be even more costly. That can cost you your entire life's work, smart financial decisions, and dreams.

TAXES

Taxes are absolutely one of the biggest threats to your finances, wealth, income, and estate goals.

This is, again, something not to shy away from or ignore. It's highly unlikely we'll see the IRS canceled or defunded in our lifetimes. In fact, we've only seen the IRS receive tens of billions of dollars in additional funding specifically for tracking down extra tax dollars and enforcing collection. With all the debt we've accumulated and changes in the economy, it is also unlikely that we'll see taxes go down by any meaningful margins in our lifetimes. Instead, there seems to be a lot of pressure to add new taxes, increase tax rates, and strip away or cap long-relied-on tax breaks.

Intelligent, wealthy individuals embrace taxes head on. They use them to get an edge and to maximize their finances, overall wealth, and multi-generational wealth. Respectively, they pay a lot less taxes, too, just by using the legal breaks and savings offered to them.

Those who stick their heads in the sand and try to ignore a tax issue, or just suck up extreme taxation, are those who end up poor or even losing everything.

Consider that on average, Americans work five or even six months each year just to pay taxes. It's called Tax Freedom Day once they reach that threshold. After that, the income you earn during the rest of the year may be used for your bills.

Of course, the more you spend on expenses, the more additional money you will spend in sales taxes.

There may be a lot you can do to earn extra money, invest for higher returns, and avoid high-interest-rate credit card debt and banking fees. Yet considering that you are probably already paying in the high double-digit percentages in taxes, any savings you can muster here can go right to your bottom line — to your savings, investment accounts, and net worth. What's great about these savings is they can be multiplied with compounding interest over the years. If you saved just $10,000 a year on taxes, that could be invested relatively easily to become more than $1M in the years ahead. That's extra, additional wealth on top of everything else you are doing. It's an incredible snowballing effect that you can't afford to miss out on. Many relatively simple tweaks to your finances can greatly decrease your tax liability each year. For example, challenging your annual property tax bill — this alone can save you thousands each year. Restructuring your income through a business entity can also often mean paying a fraction of the taxes you would on the same amount of income as an employee for someone else.

TIME

Time can also be one of the most significant threats to your finances and legacy. It can catch you off guard and work against you in various ways. But time can also be one of your best allies and tools. If you make money and time work for you, you won't have to work half as hard.

Not Being Prepared in Time

Procrastinating and putting off even the seemingly most simple and basic items can have catastrophic consequences when it comes to your legacy. Not filling out the most fundamental pieces of paper can mean throwing away your entire life's work, even if you have done everything else right and have been extremely fortunate in building massive wealth.

If you have anything at all to protect or pass on, do not wait another day to protect it. There is no guarantee you will have the ability to do it tomorrow. A few easy-to-fill-in documents can make all the difference.

If you have procrastinated in the past, understand just how high the cost of delaying this another hour is. Don't be overwhelmed by thinking you have to make everything perfect and account for every tiny detail. Instead, make a short list of the most important one to three things to do to protect your assets, and get them done. You can always expand later when you have more time.

Earned Income Ending Sooner than Expected

Most people are caught short by time. As noted in the introduction to this book, many people end up retiring years before they anticipated. Not only does this mean shaving what may be several years off the earnings and savings you planned, it also means you will be spending and living off your nest egg or passive income for more years than you planned.

While this may only be several years on average, we don't know what will happen tomorrow or next year. While we hope a financial crisis never happens, it can. No one ever expects it to happen to them, or so early. The problem can be anything from early-onset Alzheimer's to being in a car accident; long-lasting aftereffects of a virus that physically affects your ability to work; or having to take care of aging parents or a sick spouse or child.

These situations aren't always permanent, although there can be transitions or down periods between jobs, industry changes, or pandemic lockdowns. Even recessions can mean that while you may be able to work, your income may be a lot less than planned. You may have to draw on your retirement funds to pay daily bills and living expenses. Remember 2008, when millionaire CEOs suddenly had to line up to beg for minimum-wage jobs at fast-food joints.

Build a cushion into your plans, savings, and timeline to account for the unexpected. Weigh the pros, cons, and reliability of insurances to cover some of these potential gaps.

Shortened Periods of Time to Save and Invest for Retirement

In addition to earned income ending earlier than your planned timeline, other factors can affect the amount of time you have to save and invest for retirement and leaving your legacy.

Aside from large unexpected expenses, like medical bills, or being the victim of fraud, this shortened period can also be the result of poor investments with no floor, such as publicly traded stocks, stocks in private tech startups, cryptocurrencies, or NFTs — so-called investments without tangible assets or enough collateral as a safety net. That can mean having to start all over from scratch very late in life.

To catch up, you may have to dedicate a substantially higher percentage of your earned income to saving and investing in later years. In years when you may have planned to commit only 10% or zero to these accounts, you could end up having to apply 50% or more of your income to catch up. Of course, the same can be true if you waited until later in life to begin saving and investing in earnest.

Living Too Much Longer than Expected

One of the biggest threats that time presents to your plans in this context is living longer than you expect.

A long life can be a great thing. It can mean many additional years to spend with and be there for those you love and care about. It can provide much more time to compound your progress and impact. This can all be far more valuable than handing off a sizable fortune to your heirs. Of course, it is not promised. Being prepared to live much longer than you expect is equally as important for building a cushion in case your years of earning, saving, and investing are cut short.

If you only plan on living for another five years and you end up living for another 30, you will be woefully underprepared financially. You will run out of money. Instead of leaving behind a fortune, you may end up leaving behind a lot of debt and living in poverty for the last couple decades of your life. Not the inspirational legacy you want to leave behind.

This is a situation that is sadly becoming increasingly common. And it will only accelerate as life expectancy rates extend. Consider that according to the University of California-Berkeley,[1] the life expectancy for males in America was just 36.6 years old in 1918 and 42.2 years for women. That had almost doubled by 1998, to 73.8 years and 79.5 years respectively.

According to Statista,[2] South Korean women are on track for a life expectancy of 90.82 years by 2030. The National Library of Medicine[3] quotes a panel of bio-gerontologists who expect that people

1   https://u.demog.berkeley.edu/~andrew/1918/figure2.html.

2   https://www.statista.com/chart/8286/us-will-trail-other-rich-nation s-in-life-expectancy-by-2030/.

3   https://pubmed.ncbi.nlm.nih.gov/15142432/.

born in 2100 will have a median life expectancy of 100 years old, and many could live much longer than that thanks to expected leaps in antiaging technology and medicine. If your estate planning only maps out working until you are 65 and living until you are 75, that could prove to be a big problem.

BAD INVESTMENTS

While the power of time is an invaluable ally when it comes to compounding and growing your investments, passive income levels, and net worth, it doesn't mean that time will make poor investment choices any better.

This can be true of low-performing, low-return investment choices, such as bonds or precious metals. They may have some place in your overall financial plan and portfolio, but they can equally be a threat to your goals if they take up too much of that portfolio.

Then there are those investments that aren't primed or able to deliver when you need them most. Everybody loves a bull run. Bull runs in the stock market can make it hard for many to resist getting in and easy to stay in too long.

If you were heavily invested in these types of investments in 1999, 2006, or 2021, you may have felt smart and rich. Of course, if you needed that money and were counting on it to retire the following year, then you may have been crushed. Your portfolio value and net worth may have crashed by 70% or more in a matter of months. Dividends you were counting on for income could have been slashed or frozen.

Remember that this is all about ensuring things are in place when you need them, not just for 15 minutes of fame before a hard fall.

POSTHUMOUS ASSET MANAGEMENT

One of the most common issues that is more damaging than anything else is the management of assets after they are passed on. Fortunately for your peace of mind, most benefactors aren't present to witness this tragic and rapid destruction of their life's work and its aftermath for their heirs, although you may be unlucky enough to have to live it if you pass on the torch early for tax or health reasons.

You can create the perfect plan for your whole life and execute it flawlessly with every dollar and legal document. Yet that can all be burned to the ground in months due to this one factor.

As we've already discovered, leaving the most money behind or even great assets, like real estate and trust funds, isn't the silver bullet for accomplishing what you really want to do with your life. You can leave behind $20B in cash, a vault of gold bars, half of all the apartment buildings in New Jersey, or 400 acres of ranch and farmland in Texas.

How much real value, longevity, and impact that has, will all come down to how it is managed. This is even if you have aced the succession and inheritance process.

The family home is the classic example of this. So many parents believe they are making a great investment by buying their own home and spending decades paying off the mortgage, making lots of sacrifices in finances and lifestyle to leave that home for their kids. Guess what happens as soon as they die? No matter how nice the house is, and the sentimental memories it holds, it seems to be rare that children hold onto that home. Even rarer that they live in it.

What happens to that precious and well-cared-for asset? It's often sold at a fire sale price — fast for cash. The home isn't a good fit for the heirs' current lifestyles or tastes, it isn't in the right location for them, or they just see it as a lottery win that can be liquidated for cash. Some of those treasures held onto for a lifetime, like watches and rings, might be rushed off to the nearest pawnshop in the process, everything being sold for well less than it is worth.

What happens to all that free and easy money? You can bet that windfall is quickly spent and wasted in the vast majority of cases. That's probably in stark contrast to the desires of the benefactors to provide a lifelong or multi-generational asset.

This means a multi-family apartment building might be a better legacy investment than the family home. Something that has tangible value, can grow organically in value, and produces strong returns, with built-in tax breaks and even ongoing passive income. This way, heirs could have somewhere to live in a pinch, and a lifetime of income to provide for the basics and some luxuries so they can pursue their calling, without having to throw away their talents and potential just to work to support themselves.

Of course, the same thing can easily happen in this scenario: Heirs could instantly sell off and cash out an income-producing property. Without the right mindset or experience for management, they could oust long-term tenants and run the building into disrepair. They could crash the value, dry up the income, and even rack up legal bills and fines.

The way to prevent this is not to directly hand over the asset and its management entirely to those heirs. If it is handled by a professional property management company, held in a trust, or a part of a fund investment in an IRA, it could go on providing benefits as you planned for decades.

Similar analogies can be made for just about any form of investment, asset, or inheritance.

The second half of this book focuses on solving it all.

Chapter 4

FIVE VEHICLES FOR FACILITATING YOUR GOALS

"Don't be fearful of risks. Understand them, and manage and minimize them to an acceptable level."—Naved Abdali

Giving your kids a pair of chopsticks isn't going to help them get much nutrition from a bowl of clear soup, is it? You probably wouldn't expect them to hit many home runs out of a professional baseball stadium using a Nerf bat either, would you? You wouldn't expect a charity to feed many hungry kids by giving them a box full of rocks instead of canned food, right?

The same goes for empowering the legacy you want to leave. The analogies we just mentioned may seem laughable, if not cruel. Yet they illustrate just what most people end up doing financially and otherwise when they fail to use the right tools to facilitate their objectives.

Here are some important elements you may want to include in your plan and put into action immediately.

WILLS

I am not a professional tax advisor or lawyer, so it should go without saying that it is always smart to contact and use the best licensed professional experts in these fields to help with the details. Every individual's situation is unique. The details of your own plan, documents, possessions, and assets — from vehicles to properties to jewelry to funds — have to be personalized and customized as well.

It is no secret that we all need a will and last testament. The cost of not having one, especially if you have any valuable assets, is just too great (at least unless you want to mess with your potential heirs, drive them crazy, and see most of your estate lost).

It is important to note that every jurisdiction has its own rules, legal processes, and precedents. However, if you don't leave a clear and legal will, and one that is easily found or in the hands of a trusted executor, then you may take your wishes to the grave with you for eternity.

Without the presence of a will and/or other provisions and structures to guarantee your will is done, your estate will probably end up in probate. That is, when your potential heirs want to access your estate and their inheritance, they will have to find and pay for an attorney to open probate.

This can be a lengthy legal process that can include having to publish notices, attend court proceedings, have assets valued and liquidated, and settle debts before finally being able to distribute or receive any remaining proceeds. And that law firm will probably expect a percentage of whatever is left. The end result is months of stress and expense, and your heirs ultimately getting a lot less than you hoped. In many cases, your estate may not go to those you intended; if you don't have a will, your entire estate could go to a state or the federal government. Is that really the legacy you want to leave? If not, then you need a will. Don't put this off.

Make an appointment with an attorney to help you, choose an online legal service, or just put something on paper and into the right hands with a fillable form for today. You can expand on it and iron out the details with a lawyer at any point (but the sooner the better).

The important parts of this are the assets you have, whom you would like to get them and how, and who will oversee this process as your executor.

IRAS

There are many fantastic legacy advantages of leaving IRAs and similar tax-saving investment vehicles to your beneficiaries, as well as using them during your own lifetime.

Not everyone knows that IRAs can be inherited. In fact, if you just want to fast-track and supersize your investments and wealth, with serious tax advantages before your retirement, an IRA should be one of the top tools on your list.

Absolutely everyone should have one, or the equivalent of a self-directed IRA or solo 401k.

Taxes

Taxes are one of the most obvious benefits of accounts like IRAs. Some of these accounts allow for immediate tax deductions against income taxes in the year contributions are made, along with ongoing deferment of taxes on investment gains within them.

Others, like the Roth IRA, offer tax-free returns and gains. All of those double-digit-percentage tax savings can be reinvested for compounding gains.

Right here alone, you can add double digits to your net returns.

Transferring Your Wealth

Your heirs can keep an inherited IRA going as is, and not have to pay any taxes on this money at the time they inherit it. That's a great way to pass on a huge inheritance without a giant chunk being eaten up by various levels of government and taxes.

As soon as you open such an account, name your beneficiaries for rapid handover of these assets later when you pass or are incapacitated.

Funding Multiple IRAs

You might be able to set up and fund IRAs for your spouse and kids in addition to the one for yourself.

This will help you avoid any caps on individual account balances or tax savings in the future, as well as greatly multiplying the tax deductions and savings.

Teaching Your Beneficiaries the Power of Accounts

Your heirs or beneficiaries may not be in the right headspace to take your advice about using these accounts while you are still around, but by leading and showing them the power of what the accounts can do and have done, you can inspire them to keep going with these powerful tools.

Ongoing Professional Management

One of the great benefits of vehicles like these is that they automatically provide ongoing professional management and a seamless transition. You don't have to worry about your heirs destroying everything you built for them (unless they cash out the account). The nest egg can continue to be managed professionally just as you set it up.

TRUSTS

A trust is another potent vehicle and structure for estate planning, as well as growing and protecting your assets and gains during your lifetime. There are several key premises for using trusts and potential advantages of using them.

Types of Trusts

There are many types of trusts to choose from. It is wise to consult a tax professional, lawyer, and asset protection specialist to find the right types of trusts to meet your personal needs and goals. If you are already an expert on this, you can use an online service to complete your trust documents, obtain a tax ID number from the IRS online, and open a bank account for your trust online.

Types of trusts include:

- Revocable
- Irrevocable
- Education
- Spendthrift
- Charitable

- Special-needs
- Generation-skipping
- Marital
- Bypass

Your trust can acquire assets, make investments (including in real estate and mortgage notes), and receive the proceeds. You can transfer assets and funds you already have into a trust as well, or specify that certain assets and proceeds be paid into or transferred into a trust on death or incapacitation by making the trust a beneficiary of those accounts, such as life insurance, retirement, and bank accounts.

Key to making trusts work for you is choosing a trustworthy trustee and successor trustee — not only someone you can rely on, but who is capable, shares your values, will do the right thing, and can help make the most of your estate.

REAL ESTATE

Real estate is one of the most common and potentially powerful assets when thinking about your legacy.

One of the big mistakes here is thinking the home you live in is a good investment, inheritance, or legacy. This is rarely the case. Exceptions may exist, but far more often than not, this is the most wasted form of inheritance. Worse, it typically ends up becoming the biggest center of stress, dispute, and financial burden. Unless you want to financially and mentally break your beneficiaries and punish them, better options and structures exist.

However, real estate as a true investment is one of the best vehicles for empowering your legacy. For some, it is building a landmark building. For others, it has been building libraries or donating parks or conservation land. However, one of the best options is leaving income-producing real estate assets.

They are hard, tangible assets that will never go to zero. They may appreciate in value organically and benefit from value-added improvements. They can even provide passive income pretty much into infinity and for multiple generations.

This can ensure that your nest egg and capital won't be wasted, and the returns and free cash flow can be enjoyed virtually endlessly.

A variety of vehicles also can be used for holding real estate to reduce or eliminate taxes, and protecting these assets further, such as trusts and IRAs.

FUNDS

The right funds can prove to be some of the most fruitful investments when it comes to achieving your estate and legacy goals.

While many funds perform poorly, either due to being overly conservative or extremely risky, especially in the public stock market or pre-IPO tech startups, a few fantastic funds can really deliver, especially when you think in the medium to long term. The main advantage of using funds in this context is that they have professional management in place. The investing and management are done for your heirs, and in what you see as sound assets. While the underlying assets may change over time, you can trust your asset manager to make the right trades, at the right time, for wealth preservation, growth, returns, and passive income yields.

Think of it as automating investing for the next generation. This is also an equally great tool if you want to provide long-term assistance to a charity, or ensure your favorite cat is pampered for life.

Funds can also be great investments for your own lifetime by facilitating ongoing investing, wealth growth, and income during retirement or incapacitation.

You can also double up on these benefits by investing in funds through a self-directed IRA or 401k, within a trust, and in real estate investments.

If you want to actively invest yourself now, then you may also start your own fund with partners you trust. You can make it a family business (if and only if your siblings or children are really passionate and talented at this as well), or you may simply will them shares within your fund business.

Chapter 5

MAKE INTRODUCTIONS NOW

Have you talked to your kids, spouse, appointed trustees or guardians, or nonprofit charity managers about your estate and legacy goals? Introducing your beneficiaries and your financial experts now is one of the most critical actions you can take to ensure your legacy is protected and prosperous.

In fact, it is probably far, far more important than leaving anyone a single dollar, share of stock, or gold coin.

Yet not only do most people completely neglect this pivotal step, they don't even have basic financial or estate conversations with their beneficiaries.

This one factor alone can easily be directly linked to financial crises, poverty, stress, mental health challenges, and national economic performance.

START BY HAVING THE CONVERSATION

It is shocking how few actually have this conversation, although perhaps given the average person and family's financial situation, maybe it isn't so surprising.

According to a Wells Fargo survey, 72% of older Americans still keep financial matters private. Just four in 10 have family members who know how much money they have. In fact, no one else knows. Almost 60% say they see no urgency about having these conversations about their aging and money — even those in their 80s, who are often already past their life expectancy date.

These should not be subjects that are depressing or hidden. After all, these are probably the things that your life is all about — the reason you are still living, passionate, and driven.

Yet according to EZ-Probate and an Ameriprise survey, nine out of 10 people who have had conversations about their preferences for what they want to leave have only done so after a life-altering event. Waiting until you are pinned down in a horrific car wreck, high on painkillers after a heart attack in the hospital, or on your deathbed is not the time for this conversation.

That's far too late.

I hope that by the time those final months and years, or days and hours, roll around, you are prepared, your heirs and beneficiaries are well-equipped, and you can enjoy those precious, priceless moments just being together and talking about anything but money.

Planning, talking about your legacy, and charting out a bright and exciting future for yourself and your beneficiaries should be something you *want* to talk about.

It will only get brighter the more you work on it.

You don't have to tell them about every penny you have. It is understandable that you don't want to ruin your beneficiaries by making them lazy, thinking if they just wait around long enough, they'll have it made, with no effort of their own. Nor do you want vultures by your bedside, or for them to rack up so much debt in advance that it is all eaten up on transfer.

By applying many of the elements in this book, you can avoid those things and protect your legacy, while being more transparent and communicative.

You can work with your legal advisors to create and implement many clauses to protect your goals. You can insert provisions in your will that any of your heirs who become addicted to drugs must attend rehab before seeing any proceeds, or that heirs have to reach 35 or 40 years old to receive any lump sums of money.

Some people have even included language saying that any heir who tries to contest their will would be automatically disowned and receive nothing. This is in addition to wisely picking your executors and trustees, of course.

The goal is about better preparing and empowering your beneficiaries for success.

You can share asset allocation and portfolio diversification ideas, as well as some of your individual investments. For example, why you chose real estate, private lending, and funds over betting it all on Dogecoin, a fad NFT, or defaulting to the public stock market.

Even more importantly, share your values, principles, and the purpose of it all for their lifetime and beyond.

Enroll their help in coming up with ideas, testing things, and leveraging their energy to work on this. It will be far more meaningful and "sticky" if they are engaged in the process.

MAKING INTRODUCTIONS

Being intentional about making professional introductions may be even rarer than having these basic conversations about money, estate planning, and the future.

If you haven't already, you will certainly put a lot of thought, screening, testing, time, energy, and even money into finding and selecting the best professionals to work with. After all that, and proving them to be the scarce 1% in their field who are not just capable, but trustworthy, and maybe even sometimes likable, why would you give such great gifts to your beneficiaries, only to gamble on them going through the same process from scratch, and all the expensive trial and error with it? That would make zero sense, right? This is your chance to streamline and give your beneficiaries every advantage of success. If you have set things up well, then your heirs will be working with these individuals and companies anyway. If you don't make these introductions, and do it well, then that may be short-lived, along with your aspirations.

You want to be sure that these experts understand your goals and intentions during this period of your life now, for the long term, and beyond. It's extra whipped cream and chocolate drizzle on top of your frappé if they also can relate intuitively and share your passions.

Imagine you have an incredible family lawyer, who not only happens to be one of the best in the country, but is also a parent and passionate about the same charitable causes as you. They would already understand what you want to achieve, and be aligned with that. They'll have a personal connection. That is much more likely to make them care. Your kids or the cause you leave your money to won't just be another client. They will be personally invested in creating success.

Your heirs are also much more likely to pause and listen to their advice before making rash moves that could sabotage your intentions.

Who Should You Introduce?

Your lawyers are an obvious choice of professionals whom your beneficiaries should meet. The transition will be much easier if your beneficiaries already know them.

Accountants can help your beneficiaries keep a good handle on the numbers, understand where they are headed, and understand how to make the numbers work.

Even more important are introductions to your tax experts. They can have a huge impact on net transfer and how much is wasted in taxes, as well as helping your beneficiaries develop a winning tax strategy for the years ahead.

While personal relationships with bank managers and executives may be less common today, introductions to them can be important. That may earn your beneficiaries better deals on banking services, and lending when they need to borrow, as well as more leniency and breaks if they experience any struggles.

Investment advisors and asset managers certainly should be on this list. These may be professionals who are managing your investments and assets, and who you want to continue managing your trust, retirement accounts, and other assets for many years. Multi-generational relationships are valued by these professionals as well.

Remember that to succeed in anything, you don't need all the resources in the world, or to know everything yourself. You just need to know where to go for the answers; whom to ask; and how to leverage the knowledge, time, resources, and expertise of others.

Chapter 6

PUT THEM IN CHARGE OF THE MONEY

One of the most effective and powerful ways for the next generation to develop strong money and asset management skills, be empowered to make intelligent investments, and develop an appreciation for it all is to get them actively involved.

You will find this principle game-changing.

The results can be absolutely jaw-dropping, even in heirs who you think are lazy, wasteful, uninterested, or irresponsible. Once they are in charge of the money you leave, and the wins or losses, they can't help but be more interested, motivated, and compelled to make better money choices.

No matter how fearful you are about how they will do with this responsibility, there are methods that work almost regardless of age.

It is far better for them to make little mistakes now and learn from that — to lose $10 or $100 now, with plenty of time to learn and make it up — before you hand off a larger inheritance and more responsibility.

TEST ACCOUNTS

Test accounts are a very low-risk way to get others started. They are great for teaching basic principles, instilling appreciation for missing out on opportunities, and even making investing and money management fun through gamification. Kids as young as five years old can get into this. In fact, it is a great way to augment their schooling.

A variety of stock-trading simulation tools are available on the web. You don't have to use real money, but you can use these tools to show your beneficiaries what they would have made or lost based on their choices. You can even make it more fun by offering a prize to compete for.

You may not want to push them in the direction of publicly traded stocks. If real estate is your thing, you can always easily show them how to track home values and rents online. Let them pick a few different types of properties and track how values and cash flow might change over time.

For those you feel are too young for this, board games like Monopoly and the Game of Life can be ways to teach about money and life choices.

BANK ACCOUNTS AND CREDIT CARDS

At some point, you need to teach your kids about bank accounts and credit cards. Again, it is probably better for them to make mistakes with your supervision than to make blunders with harsh, longer-term consequences, like overdraft fees, negative credit issues, and more.

Many banks offer child and teen accounts. Some can be opened with a few clicks online. Your kids can feel a great sense of pride from holding their own bank cards, and ordering and paying for purchases themselves.

Unfortunately, these accounts are not always cheap. Monthly fees can be hefty, as can other transaction and service fees. This in itself may be a good lesson.

Alternatively, you can use jars or envelopes at home to separate cash. You can divide them by general spending, giving, general savings, and savings for specific goals (such as a vacation at Disney World or buying a new VR setup).

This can illustrate how quickly savings can add up and help your beneficiaries develop a sense of accomplishment.

You'll probably also notice a huge change in their mindset, especially when it comes to spending. Spending quickly becomes more painful when they have to use their own money. They'll often realize they don't need things so badly when it means dipping into their own accounts to make purchases.

You might consider offering parent-paid interest to add to the motivation to save and teach them about compound interest, or some sort of savings matching for something big, like a first car.

When your beneficiaries do spend their own money, they'll probably be more careful about what they buy. If they buy a phone or laptop, they probably won't be so careless with it or throw it around when they'll have to sacrifice to save up for a new one.

This is a great time to introduce allowances, or even better, work and business. If you don't want to give your kids an allowance and teach them to be dependent on free money, then you can start with giving them a list of daily and weekly chores to do to earn the allowance.

You can set them up with a PayPal account and get a mobile reader so they can sell things and collect payments; put money in the bank for mowing lawns and washing neighbors' cars; or be more entrepreneurial and sell lemonade, firewood, or collectibles in person and online.

CREATE A FAMILY BANK

About the only thing old-school banks seem good for these days is as a source to buy discounted properties (REOs) and mortgage loan notes as investments. Otherwise, they are just one of the biggest expenses your beneficiaries will find are eating up your inheritance, and one of the biggest risks in bleeding negative returns or fraud when it comes to building your legacy.

It is far better to set up your own family bank.

You can use it for lending, borrowing, credit, and more. Family members and others may borrow from your capital, then pay back origination fees and interest. You can let your heirs evaluate and make credit decisions.

They'll learn to evaluate borrowing and business ideas pretty quickly, and will realize it if one of their siblings is highly unlikely to repay a loan.

Instead of paying fees and interest to another bank or lender, that money can accumulate in your own family bank. Building your nest egg, instead of depleting it.

Consider how much this could add up between startup businesses, cars, college, houses, and investments. You could even set up a family trust early and have your heirs vote on how to use and manage the funds.

This gives them the experience of ownership and helps them learn to work together, navigate mistakes, and enjoy wins together

FAMILY GIFTS

These various ventures can also be funded with financial gifts. To avoid heftier taxes later, you can begin divesting your inheritance now.

The IRS offers an annual gift tax exemption. For 2022, that was $16,000 per individual, up $1,000 from the previous year. The annual cap is per person and annual gifts under this amount can avoid transfer taxes, so you could give five children $15,999 per year each to invest and avoid the transfer taxes.

If giving a child or other beneficiary that whole amount at once is a financial stretch at any given point, then it could be done in tandem with holidays and birthdays — financial gifts that you may give in cash, or deposit into retirement or investment accounts, that add up to the annual cap.

This tax break should continue to change as inflation goes up, although dragging your feet on it could also mean that it is stripped away in the future by a pro-tax government administration.

A lifetime cap also applies. That was just over $12M in 2022.

REWARD SYSTEMS

Having your kids or heirs do the math and see that continuing to save, invest, and apply these principles can make them millionaires, or at least far wealthier over time, may be quite inspiring to some. Others will need more rapid and tangible rewards to keep them excited.

While the best investments may not be the most exciting ones, at this stage, getting your beneficiaries interested and engaged may be most important. This may require both providing quick rewards that anchor successful money management in their minds and motivate them, as well as allowing for a budget to invest in some things you typically wouldn't invest in, but that could make all the difference in engaging them. That in turn can create great learning moments, with a safety net.

Find out what your beneficiaries are interested in, and look for ways to let them invest in those interests. Teenagers, especially, can be in tune with the latest trends. If they spend a lot of time on YouTube, allow them to buy a share of Alphabet stock. It's great when you can get physical share certificates to put on the wall — that makes it tangible. The same goes for some of their favorite brands, whether it's stock in a shoe, game, or their dream car brand.

It could be trending types of investments, like NFTs or crypto. It doesn't hurt to let them put in $100 or buy a single share in something, learn how to track it, and choose when to sell it.

You could allow them to buy a piece of real estate, or even a franchise of their favorite store. This, again, can show them how to think like an owner and investor rather than a worker.

When it comes to rewards, these have to be applicable to the people involved. They should combine both quick hits of positive chemicals in the brain and instill the balance of hustle and patience it takes to manage money successfully.

This could be as simple as taking the kids out for ice cream or pizza when you acquire a new property, or saving some of the cash flow and yields from investments to buy a new gaming laptop.

This isn't just about kids, either. For older beneficiaries, rewards could include things like new designer outfits, jewelry, vacations, etc.

Chapter 7

TEACH THEM

Simply giving money is rarely the best way to empower a meaningful and lasting legacy, or to have any solid impact for that matter.

It may be far better to give someone $300 and the know-how for what to do with it rather than $300M and no idea how to manage it well.

If your kids or beneficiaries know how to use such a gift, they will flourish no matter what. In the reverse, it doesn't matter how many zeros there are; it will quickly fall apart without knowledge and understanding.

Teaching them — equipping them with what they need to know — is not only one of the best gifts you can give, but also the best way to actually empower others for success.

The optimal methods to accomplish this can vary distinctly by the individual, their age, and other factors. It can also fall into two distinct categories: mindset and practical skills.

What are some of the ways to teach the value of saving and how to manage investments, either now or after you're gone?

BOOKS

The successful and wealthy read. I've never met or heard of anyone who has been truly successful and kept their wealth who doesn't read. In fact, there seems to be a direct correlation between how many hours each day people read and their level of wealth and success. Success not only leaves clues, but the successful willingly share their secrets in these books. It is the best way to hack decades and centuries of knowledge.

Depending on the relationship, you could leverage this by reading together, giving books, or leaving a library behind after you are gone.

This book itself could be instrumental in helping your beneficiaries empower their own future legacies. If you have procrastinators among your heirs, check out *The Tire Kicker*. Everyone should have a copy of *The Timeless Principles of Investing in Real Estate* in their homes and offices. Other fundamental books may include *The Guide to Diversifying in Real Estate* as well as *Think and Grow Rich* and *Rich Dad Poor Dad*.

ALTERNATIVES TO BOOKS

Books are unique, especially physical books. Yet not everyone is ready to read. There are ways to supplement this in the meantime, and also instill the same ideas, if only subconsciously.

Podcasts and audiobooks are probably the most obvious. You can give them and share links to them on a regular basis. You could even leave a specially curated playlist and digital library.

Even better, you can let these things play when you are together — if you are commuting together or taking a road trip. You can play them at home during your morning power hour, or instead of binging on TV in the evenings. You might be surprised at how much your kids and heirs soak in passively. It may even prompt some great conversations.

Videos have also become popular. If that's what it takes to get their attention and engagement for now, then include videos.

Taking online courses and classes together can also have benefits, as can attending live seminars and events.

You can fund their tuition, although doing it together creates a team bond. Some people are very social by nature and need these more interactive environments to keep up their interest and engagement.

Another very powerful element of this process is not telling them what to do or think. It doesn't matter if you have their best interests at heart, know what is best for them, and just want to help. Some people are just naturally resistant. They won't listen.

That can be an especially strong reaction between parent and child, at least until the child reaches a certain age. They are much more likely to copy what you do than what you say. Some will be much more receptive to a third party giving them the same information.

You may have tried to convey something for years. They resisted and dismissed it.

Then someone else says it, and they think it is genius and bring it to you as their idea. The point is that they get it, by any means necessary.

Putting your beneficiaries in the seat to hear the same advice you offer from someone else and learn from them can be very powerful. Then this knowledge can take on a life of its own. It can be self-motivating for them.

OTHER FORMS OF EDUCATION

Training is most effective when you can combine and show how to apply passions and talents in a way that is both enjoyable and profitable, as well as when offered in the way that someone learns best. Some of us absorb much better visually, some via audio and listening, and others by doing.

Perhaps you are not a big believer in conventional education and college and student debt — but they might be. It may be their thing. Could you offer to pay for some college credits if they include classes on entrepreneurship, or a class or two at a top school like Harvard where they can benefit from networking?

If they don't take well to conventional schooling with textbooks or online lectures, can you get them an internship? That could be with a real estate developer, where they can learn more about real estate investing. It could be with a fund and trading firm to learn more about investing, while earning their own money.

Chapter 8

TRAIN THEM

Instilling knowledge and the right mindset will be invaluable for empowering a great legacy and the success of the next generation. This is true regardless of how much or little you have to pass on.

However, there is also no substitute for practical, hands-on skills and experience.

There are 10- and 16-year-olds who have bought and remodeled real estate, or who have built international companies online with many employees. They are typically far ahead of those who have gone through years of college and may have an MBA but zero real-world experience.

When it comes to empowering your legacy, it's far more effective to pass on not only knowledge, but training and real experience, too.

There are ways to do this for every age, type of talent, and interest.

Here are some ideas you could try, or use as brainstorming to come up with your own.

It's all about finding interesting ways to engage, teach, and equip others that work for them.

RAISING YOUR KIDS TO BE INVESTORS AND ENTREPRENEURS

Even at their youngest ages, you can begin training your kids to invest in things like real estate. Many times, these early training sessions are the ideal way to fuel that legacy, while being able to enjoy more quality time together with those you love and working on things you both care about.

When your kids are at the youngest ages, you can drive around neighborhoods on the weekends and have them spot For Sale signs, or point out houses that may be abandoned. You can do this when on your way to and from the park for playtime. If they score some points, you might end your drive by stopping for a treat or their favorite snack. You let them pick and play a victory theme song in the car while you all sing along in celebration.

At the grocery store, you can have your kids compete to find the best-value deals on items on your list. Teach them how to compare value. Let them earn a percentage of the savings they find to spend on a toy or game they've been wanting.

You can train them how to evaluate properties and other assets as well. In real estate, this could involve taking photos of properties with their phones, then running down a printed or mobile checklist of qualifying factors.

You can let them walk through inspection reports.

If you are considering buying businesses, you can evaluate things like foot traffic, customer service, and quality of products.

Even before they hit 10 years old, kids have a lot of common sense and can pretty easily distinguish rip-offs from great businesses.

That's often far more telling than all the volumes of junk data and graphs that financial analysts geek out over and publish.

When it comes to closing deals, don't let them sit off to the side or in the waiting room, watching TikTok on their phones while you interact with the client. Have them dress for success and sit with you at the conference table. That will train the people you work with to start respecting your kids and future heirs as decision-makers. And if the kids want to get paid, they should be there when you're closing the deal, so they can learn what's involved.

When it comes to fixing and flipping houses or rehabbing apartment buildings, they can paint and carry materials. They can write and put out For Sale signs. Take pictures to document their activity and contributions.

INSTILLING A PASSION FOR IMPORTANT CAUSES

Aside from the business and investing side of your legacy, there is a lot that you can train your heirs in when it comes to charitable giving and causes, too.

Even preteens can help with fundraising efforts for nonprofit causes. These can be to support larger organizations or your own charitable ventures. They can go door to door, use social media and crowdfunding platforms online, or sell lemonade in the neighborhood.

You can find time to volunteer and actively participate in causes you both care about. If you care about the environment, you can plant trees together. You can adopt animals. You can participate in local cleanup projects. You can build houses together, dedicate parks and green space, or give someone a job. You could also brainstorm and have them help hold you accountable for how you use things around the home, what you buy, and which companies you choose to do business with.

You can even start your own nonprofit and dedicate a part of the proceeds from your investments and businesses to it.

TRAINING OTHERS

Even if you don't have kids, there may be others you plan to pass on the baton of your legacy to. That may be a spouse, siblings, nephews and nieces, or people in your community you want to help. Again, this is about finding their talents and interests, and ways to apply them.

Maybe they can be property scouts who can bring you deals. This will give you the opportunity to train them in what's a good deal — a property worth buying, or not.

If they are creative, then perhaps they can help you with design for your marketing materials. Or even your social media feed. Even a five-year-old can learn to build websites.

Some people may not gravitate to the business and numbers side of things yet. You can still find ways to make it work. For real estate investments, they might be great at picking out remodeling and decorating materials.

Maybe they are super-social beings and thrive on interaction with others. They could host open houses; go networking with you; enjoy dining out while you do deals; or leverage their social media networks to find buyers, sellers, and financial partners.

If they are into art, collectibles, fashion, or luxury, then try to engage them by going to view dream houses, attending fashion shows, and visiting art galleries and auctions. These can be opportunities to acquire assets, advertise, network, sell, invest, and learn more about asset classes.

Chapter 9

MAKE WISE, FUTURE-PROOF INVESTMENTS NOW

It is critical to begin making the right investments now to facilitate the future and legacy you want to live and leave.

Working through this book, you should have gained more clarity about what you want and need, as well as the gaps between what you have and the trajectory you are on versus where you need to get to, along with some of the important vehicles to help you get there and realize your goals and objectives.

We've even covered a variety of practical ideas for equipping your beneficiaries to get the most out of any assets you leave them.

Now it's time to tackle what's most important in investing to get you there — for covering yourself while you are still here, making the most of the time you have, and leaving the most you can in the most efficient and safest way.

SEVEN KEY INVESTING PRINCIPLES FOR MAXIMIZING YOUR LEGACY

1. Passive income
2. High, risk-adjusted returns for safe growth
3. Tax protections
4. Asset protection
5. Diversification
6. Seamless ongoing management
7. Ability to weather ups, downs, and turnovers when you need to

Passive Income

To avoid burning through any savings, investment capital, or assets you already have, you need passive income. It is also vital for creating more surplus capital to invest and reinvest. Setting up ongoing passive cash flow can also be critical for facilitating your long-term legacy objectives for your beneficiaries.

A substantial part of your investment portfolio and asset allocation should be geared toward generating passive income.

High-Return, Risk-Adjusted Investments

You want your savings, investments, and nest egg to keep on growing for you. Subpar — 4% or 5% — returns just won't cut it. They may barely take a small bite out of how negative you are going.

Of course, just swinging for the fences and going all in on extremely risky bets can wipe you out even faster. The promise of a 70% return is worthless if you end up losing all your capital, and get zero returns.

The key is risk-adjusted returns — returns that are balanced by the risks involved. Although you should also demand strong returns from your investments.

Tax Protections

As we've already determined, taxes are one of the biggest and most significant threats to your finances and legacy goals.

It is vital to seek out investments with plenty of tax advantages — like real estate — as well as to use a variety of layers of tax-saving vehicles. These can include self-directed IRAs, business entities, 1031 exchanges, and more. Don't forget trusts, wills, gifts, and other tools for minimizing taxes on transfer.

Asset Protection

Protecting your gains is as important as making them. There is no sense in hitting big wins if you let it all slip away before you really need it.

Trusts, business entities, retirement accounts, professional asset management, and other tools can help increase privacy and add additional layers of protection from malicious lawsuits and criminals.

This is also about picking the right investments.

There are many investments advertised, and even, sadly, many very common ones with no floor and no downside protection. NFTs, crypto, publicly traded stocks, and private stocks in tech startups are classic examples of this. You can lose everything and have nothing to bounce back with. You'll be starting from scratch again. That may be rare in public stocks, but it isn't uncommon to lose 50% to 70% of your asset value in a matter of hours or weeks in some other types of investments.

It is understandable to let yourself gamble with some funds for the chance of some lucky wins. Some will cling to overly conservative investments like bonds, CDs, and precious metals (which may not always be as safe as you think), although that can hold back your overall finances due to their slow growth and small returns.

Dabbling in a few of these things with a small percentage of your money may make you feel good. Just don't let it hold you back, or confuse it with actually being safe. Ideally, you'll find assets with hard tangible value that provide a foundation and downside protection.

They'll never go to zero, and can bounce back, with good expectations of strong upside returns — even better if they have the ability to keep on generating passive income cash flow, regardless of any temporary value fluctuations.

Diversification

Diversification is key for consistently and predictably generating passive income, maintaining wealth, achieving healthy and sustainable growth, and ensuring you are always covered when you need to be.

Reaching those goals requires both deep and broad diversification. It requires intelligent diversification, not just spreading your money all over the place for the sake of variety.

You want a balanced portfolio that will always have assets that are firing on all cylinders; plenty of cover for unprecedented events; assets that offer leaps in wealth, passive cash flow, downside protection, and more. That may include rental properties, flipping houses, investing in mortgage loan notes, using tax liens, and more.

I strongly urge you to read my book about intelligent diversification to make sure you are doing this well, and don't fall into the common traps that the vast majority of investors make.

Seamless Ongoing Management

While you may enjoy actively investing and being involved in making money moves early on, even well into your 70s, it is vital to have passive income and succession plans in place, as well as facilitate the seamless ongoing management of the bulk of your investments and wealth well before you need it. That day could come in 40 years, or today.

Self-directed retirement accounts and trusts that are invested in professionally managed funds are perfect for this.

Weather Ups, Downs, and Turnovers When You Need to

You don't want to be that next tragic riches-to-rags headline in the tabloids. You don't want all you've built up to all fall apart just at the wrong moment.

The answer is future-proofing your money, investments, and legacy.

Have you future-proofed your finances yet?

It may sound so obvious to do, but almost no one does. The vast majority of investments being advertised decade after decade aren't designed to be future-proofed. They are designed to be fads — just something new to sell you on and make a commission on this month.

I've seen and experienced these swings and their financial impacts — everything from great recessions, to bubbles and busts, natural disasters, pandemics, and lockdowns.

I decided I wasn't going to allow these things to derail my own legacy and the plans I have for my future, the ability to take care of those I love and contribute to important causes, or the legacy I want to leave for my kids.

That is why I created NNG Capital and pioneered the concept of the hybrid fund: a diversified fund investment that is designed to help others future-proof their money and legacy. You can check it out online and see how it works. You can try to replicate the same ideas for yourself, or you may even want to try it out and see how much of a difference it can make for you and those you love.

Chapter 10

CREATE YOUR TO-DO LIST

You should now have a much clearer idea of the kind of legacy you want to create, and what you need to do to make it a reality.

As we found out in Chapter 3, one of the biggest threats to your hopes, goals, and best-laid plans is *not* taking action. This is where you gain control and make it happen; where you go from nice ideas and average results to actually making things happen and empowering a great legacy. We've covered several steps to get from zero to hero in this book. Where you need to jump in depends on where you are on your journey right now. **These action items include the following:**

1. Set Specific, Tangible Goals and Objectives

List your most important objectives to act as your decision guide and North Star for everything else. Flip back to Chapter 1 if you need some help with this.

2. Understand the Gap

If you haven't done so yet, perform the exercise in Chapter 2. Evaluate where you are now in terms of your finances, trajectory, protection of your estate, and equipping your beneficiaries. Compare that to where you want and need to be. Identify the gaps and where you need to make some tweaks or take some new action.

Note any critical items you are missing, such as wills, self-directed retirement accounts, better accountants to help you save on taxes, etc. Bullet-point or number these items on your to-do list to take immediate action on.

3. Start Empowering Your Heirs

List one to three things you can do this week to empower your beneficiaries to manage and get the most out of your legacy. This may be making introductions, gifting books, finding a teachable moment, or encouraging them to take up an entrepreneurial project. Refer back to this book for more ideas to build on as you go.

4. Make Intelligent Investments

Whether you are just starting out saving and investing, or already have several million in your portfolio and realize that it just isn't going to cut it, decide to take action on making the right investments right now.

You may benefit from tax-loss harvesting on investments that are down right now. You may also get tax breaks this year by switching it up now. Whether you have $100 or $100,000 you can invest or shift right now, find an investment you can make today that will put you on the right track and move you closer to where you want to be.

PUTTING IT INTO ACTION

Make this short action list for success. All you need to begin is those one to four items.

Champion them immediately.

Reward yourself and celebrate that.

Then use that momentum to keep on building on it.

Conclusion

Thanks and congratulations on getting and making it through this book! I trust you have discovered at least a few great nuggets you can use to both build an even greater legacy in your lifetime and empower what you want most to happen well after you've handed on the torch.

I'm confident that if you start putting these actions into play, you will see great progress and be far more certain that you are on the right track and things are taken care of. You should be able to enjoy much more peace on a daily basis, and be far more excited about life and what each week holds for you.

I can't wait to see what you create and build, and how that continues to grow and grow!

About the Author

Investor, wealth manager, educator, and proud father of two incredibly financially savvy sons, Fuquan Bilal has spent more than 21 years operating businesses and perfecting his proprietary formulas for investing in real estate and other alternative asset classes.

When he's not in the office, you might catch Fuquan running to the gym, experimenting with new tweaks to his personal performance, taking on new challenges, exploring new markets with his kids, or hosting the Passion for Real Estate Investments (PFREI) podcast.

As the founder and chief visionary officer of NNG Capital Fund, Fuquan has proven to deliver to investors through a variety of funds over the years, most notably when it comes to providing attractive risk-adjusted returns and achieving predictable levels of passive income — all born of his passion for helping others future-proof their finances and create their own legacies.

He is one of the few leaders in this arena who has proven to come through and level up through periods of national and global economic distress *and* prosperity.

What may really separate Fuquan from others, in addition to his magnetic personality, is the care he has for sustainably managing his clients' funds, as well as managing his teams and treating them well, and caring about the communities where his firms operate.

While these may seem fluffy to some, they are absolutely the differentiator when it comes to survival and the ability to thrive for companies, funds, and reputations, and all of those counting on them.

If you haven't yet, be sure to catch up on Fuquan Bilal's first four books (available on Amazon): *Turning Distress into Success,* about how to navigate tough markets; *The Tire Kicker,* about taking action; *The Guide to Diversifying in Real Estate for the Intelligent Real Estate Investor;* and *The Timeless Principles of Investing in Real Estate: The Keys to Building Real Wealth and Keeping it.*

About NNG

NNG Capital Fund is an alternative investment firm specializing in real estate assets and mortgage debt investments for passive investors.

Originally born as a solution for the inefficiencies that Fuquan Bilal experienced in the investment arena and to invest his own capital more wisely and profitably, NNG's series of funds have proven incredibly popular with other sophisticated investors as well.

NNG Capital offers access to superior investments with industry-leading performance, accountability, and transparency.

The firm is built on timeless investment principles, while consistently embracing innovation and constantly striving for greater results. It is built on shared successes, intelligent investing, and an openness to finding better ways to do things. It's about investing safely and more profitably, while treating everyone the company touches the way they ought to be.

www.ingramcontent.com/pod-product-compliance
Lightning Source LLC
Chambersburg PA
CBHW071439210326
41597CB00020B/3863